GROWING:

In Finding Me, I Found Wholeness"

**By:
Lashawndra Robinson**

Copyright @2023 by Lashawndra Robinson

All rights reserved. No part of this publication may be reproduced, stored in a retrieval system, or transmitted in any form or by any means electronic, mechanical, photocopying, recording, or otherwise without the written permission of the authors.

Limits of Liability-Disclaimer

The authors and publisher shall not be liable for your misuse of this material. The purpose of this book is to educate and empower. The authors and/or publisher do not guarantee that anyone following these techniques, suggestions, tips, ideas, and/or strategies will become successful.

The authors and/or publisher shall have neither liability nor responsibility to anyone concerning any loss or damage caused or alleged to be caused directly or indirectly by the information contained in this book.

ISBN: 978-1-957522-08-1
Published By: InspiredByVanessa
www.InspiredByVanessa.com

TABLE OF CONTENTS

Dedication 1

Introduction 3

Chapter 1: *Intentionality* 9

Chapter 2: *Learning and Growing* 33

Chapter 3: *Your Only Limit is You* 51

Chapter 4: *Forgive Yourself* 70

Chapter 5: *The New Thing* 86

Conclusion 108

References 116

About the Author 118

DEDICATION

I would like to, first and foremost, give thanks to God. God has shined his marvelous light on me, and for that, he genuinely gets all the glory for the glory over my life.

To myself, you decided to pick up your cross and carry it, and I am proud of you. With submission and discipline, you have broken generational behaviors. I love you.

For my village and to every soul I've encountered along the way to becoming, I'm grateful. Our many experiences and relationships have helped shape the trajectory of the now, which is a part of my story, my journey, and my DNA. It helped create lines in the blueprint that had been set before me. Thank you.

It is true to whom much is given, much is required. With every talent entrusted to me, I have strived to use it to glorify God, so the call continues to be a faithful and wise manager.

Greater power does come with greater responsibility, so I pray that God continues to empower me with his strength amid any human weaknesses.

I pray that I continue to remain dedicated. I pray that my talents, wealth, knowledge, love, and wisdom will be increased throughout my lifetime.

Always remember, Lashawndra, you are not alone, Breathe.

INTRODUCTION

It all goes back to childhood...

As a young girl, I grew up in a time when the family business was sacred. It was a rule that still exists in many family households today: no matter what happens inside the family home, you are not to let it leave out. It goes like this, "What goes on in this house, Stays in this House." As you evolve, you learn that some things put into place to protect others would create dysfunctional adult perspectives in almost every relational aspect of our lives. This one rule has manifested so many childhood traumas that cannot be undone. It has created a generational cycle of making the voice of children, women, and men voiceless.

I met and connected with a sister in Christ one day, who would later become a mentor, friend, and confidant, and she mentioned these words, "the devil's secrets." When we sat down for lunch, and I shared how my voice didn't matter in my marriage and how I didn't want to do life anymore, her gentle response was, "You do not have to do life alone; don't be keeping the devil's secrets." The devil's secrets can be any information categorized to keep you depressed, distressed, and disconnected. Sometimes, our mind tells us that sharing personal information could stir some stuff up and potentially worsen things in our lives or others.

Why was I so afraid to share with anyone outside of my home that I was going through domestic violence in my perceived happy marriage?

As a beautiful, striving young lady, why was I tormented with having no voice in my relationships? Not even at work. As a great mother to most, why was I my child's worst inner voice?

How could I give everyone else advice that helped put their life together, yet mine kept falling apart?

Where do I go from here with all these accolades I do not desire to use or pursue?

These questions plagued my mind, yet learned childhood behaviors, reality, and culture made it too shameful to express aloud. Social Media only existed after my adolescence, so the only outlet of information I was exposed to was neighborhood friends and a whiff of adult conversations. Even today, in the 21st Century, adult women, both young and old, do not openly or rarely privately speak about things that we as women go through personally.

Are you ready to break this Generational Cycle? Your children and their children will triumph because of your decisions today!

Our testimony is someone else's miracle, but only if we share it. God commands us not to forsake the assembly of one another, for iron truly, sharpens iron. That command should apply at home, in business, and in your personal life. Having an impact on anyone's life comes with a level of sacrifice. Your seed of sacrifice will produce a harvest for Breakthroughs, Miracles, and Healing for those you are connected to and those you don't know.

No matter how solid and independent we are, we will need to lean on someone outside of ourselves at some point in this life. I have learned and experienced that I do not have to remain in a sunken bubble alone until it pops. I believe the same for you.

God has a way of showing us that we can share life with people as human as we are. We have brothers and sisters in Christ who share a heart of love and want to see others win, grow, and become all God has called us to be.

The village required to raise kids does not exempt adults from needing a village to help navigate life's journey. You do not have to do it all alone. It is about stepping out of our safe comfort zones and Making the Connections.

So, I write this book for every woman who may face or has faced challenges in life that have made her think beyond the now while sometimes crying in despair, yet you know that there must be something more significant on the horizon if I could Press Through.

Anticipate the moments when your salt and light help change the world. Moments where

Love is a mere whisper of a voice Proclaiming to your inner self, I am ready to be Molded into The Woman God Has Ordained for Me to Be and Pursue My Purpose.

Always remember, Your voice matters!

CHAPTER 1:
INTENTIONALITY

As I went through therapy, it was evident that I had faulty childhood behaviors that attributed to me living in what would later be called survival mode. A mode where I was always looking for the next season of turbulence and even creating it myself. It was like, a sense of always protecting myself so I couldn't be hurt. During those survival seasons, other people were hurt; that was never intended to be. It's true; hurt people do hurt people. As I unlearned those behaviors, I had to forgive myself. Forgive me for doing the best I knew how to. I also had to pray that

God helps to heal those I had hurt and that they would forgive me too. In contacting some of those I hurt, I realized I could not right all wrongs or mistakes I've made in my lifetime.

Events in life can bring about an optimistic or pessimistic perspective based on life experiences. The universe is always neutral about any happenings around you, although your mind classifies these happenings as either good or bad. Your mind chooses to process or interpret things in those connotations because there are elements of fear and error within us. Your mind even perceives some obstacles as setbacks, resulting in feelings of defeat, vs. it will all work out for your good. We can decide if anything can impede our growth and development in our lives or not.

The human mind has been studied and seen to be a mind that exaggerates dangers a lot without considering looking at them from a positive or more extensive viewpoint. An example is when you are hurt by something; your mind focuses on what you have lost, which causes you to regurgitate the sad emotions you would naturally feel. This results in feelings of wanting to give up instead of giving it another shot.

If you can take a moment and look back over your life, you will see that the bad experiences helped you appreciate the value of the tremendous and positive experiences. When you feel beat down, it is not the time to give up and turn to negative labeling. Dwelling in negativity affects your mindset about life so naturally that you will find it challenging to think positively.

To upset this way of thinking and have a positive impact, seize the opportunity to prove to yourself that you will get better at this. This will boost productivity in your journey.

God designs life to be a puzzle, and He is the only one who can put the pieces together so that it makes sense. No matter one's mindset, I've discovered that God's plan and design are far better than anyone can come up with themselves. Therefore, we must live according to God's plan rather than our own. Every moment we live apart from God's plan is an opportunity wasted.

Do you want to move from emptiness to fullness, brokenness to wholeness, and meaninglessness to a life of purpose?

Are you someone that hasn't been living intentionally?

This chapter is intended to clear your doubt and enable you to see the bigger picture in the perfect and purposeful plan God has created for a life of living intentionally.

I want to take this opportunity to share how partnering with God, stepping out of my comfort zone, and connecting with others helped me discover myself and my purpose.

I vividly remember standing in front of my bathroom after a good crying worship, and I asked God, "**Who am I?**"

God responded with, "You are Precious." From that moment on, I decided to be intentional about everything that involved my transformation.

Intentional living is a personalized decision that will guide your life toward God's will, plan, and purpose for your life.

Intentional living, therefore, is living for God, the plans of God, and the mission of God. It gives you daily purpose, bringing you much closer to your creator, who knows precisely what is best for your life and no one else.

According to Joshua 24:14-15, *"Now, therefore, fear the Lord and serve him in sincerity and truth; remove the gods your ancestors served on the other side of the river and in Egypt, and serve the Lord. If it is unacceptable in your sight to serve the Lord, choose for yourselves this day whom you will serve: whether the gods which your ancestors served in the region beyond the river or the gods of the Amorites in whose land you are living. Still, as for me and my household, we will serve the Lord."*

This Bible text tells of man's duty, which is to serve God, as this is the whole duty of man. When we commit our lives to God, we receive a reason to live, and his works begin to work in our hearts to reveal his true character and will in us and through us.

"Do not conform to the pattern of this world but be transformed by the renewing of your mind. Then, you will be able to test and approve what God's will is- his good, pleasing, and perfect will." Roman 12:2

Earthly currency is unstable and fleeting. Your heavenly treasures do not lie there. Treasure is anything we value above all else and motivates us to action. Wherever your treasure is, your heart follows.

Our lives are a constant stream of many choices and decisions. More than ever, options come at us from all sides to distract us, so moments of *self-reflection* and *refocus* are a must.

How intentionally are you living today?

In that thought of reflection, know that we all have work to do, for *'everyone sins and falls short of God's glorious standard.'*

Your relationship with God is truly your most important priority in this life. It is the foundation from which you build everything else. Love God with all your heart, mind, and soul with the entirety of your strength. Everything else falls into place when God is in the proper position in our lives, including relationships, business, and home.

Planning to live a life of intentionality

In living a life of intentionality, there's the need for you to plan for your future. Writing the vision and making it plain is the goal.

1. Change your attitude, for you have a new mind in Christ Jesus.
2. Make better decisions based on your renewed mind.
3. Find inner happiness to live with little or no regrets.
4. Find your distinct purpose by identifying what God is speaking to your soul.
5. Allow your purpose to shape your life.

Living intentionally is purposeful rather than allowing life to happen to us.

4 Main Obstacles
of Living Intentionally

In my pursuit of intentionality, hindrances were found.

1. Comfort Zone – Seeking after what God put on our souls will pull us out of our present safe place. Our future will look like our present with the unwillingness to get out of our usual range of familiarity. Trusting God helps you to break free from that comfort zone.
2. Fear – Fear is a hoodlum! It incapacitates us with falsehoods and discloses that we will sink if we get out of the boat. However, when we get out of the boat, Jesus is there to grasp our hands and make the unthinkable a reality.
3. Misunderstanding 'Being Still' – Being still isn't sitting back, becoming idle, and waiting on God. In the stillness, it

is the time to renew your mind while enduring the present and standing on God's word vs. what's in front of you. Feeding your <u>spirit</u> more than your <u>stomach</u> in that season would be best.
4. Misunderstanding of the Sovereignty of God – God is sovereign; however, this doesn't imply that He will make every decision for us. In His power and creation, He has given us a choice. We decide whether to follow His voice and carry on or do our own thing. It is a relationship, not a dictatorship.

The Church ought to be comprised of the most purposeful individuals on earth. God has addressed us all somehow about His plans for our lives. We should not pause timelessly and let life happen to us but instead, be deliberate about seeking His will for our lives. Hebrews 11:6 discloses that confidence satisfies God and that He is the rewarder of the people who gravitate toward Him.

Setting Goals

I never used to set goals. I would plan everything out in my head and work it from there. I would surely forget some steps, and low and behold, stumbling took place. Setting goals is essential to intentional living. Now, I like to make plans and set goals, but I also want to leave room to be spontaneous. Goal setting included me aligning my energy with my desire so that it manifests into something tangible. Writing down my dreams and passions by creating a vision board periodically or using old-school pencil and paper geared me towards provisions set before me for things to be made plain.

I don't know where you stand, and there's certainly not one correct way to manage your time, but if you are struggling with prioritizing your time and activities, ask yourself if what you're doing is accomplishing God's will in your life or self-desires. If you're not sure, take it to him in prayer. He's longing to point you in the right direction. God must be the starting point of all goal alignment.

God doesn't want us to be lazy and slothful in our dealings. Check out Proverbs 6:6-11, *"Take a lesson from the ants, you lazybones. Learn from their ways and become wise! Though they have no prince or governor or ruler to make them work, they labor hard all summer. Gathering food for the winter. But you, lazybones, how long will you sleep? When will you wake up? A little extra sleep, a little more slumber, a little folding of the hands to rest – then poverty will pounce on you like a bandit; scarcity will attack you like an armed robber.*

Planning your goals in a way designed with intentionality ultimately impacts you positively and the individuals around you. It's not about being perfect every day. It's about making commitments stimulating from setting goals and progressing towards the rise and fall; in the pursuit of intentional living. When you live every day with the mindset "I'm on my way," you'll be more willing to embrace every part of your journey, the highs, and the lows.

Relationships and Intentionality

We can live intentionally with and through our relationships in several ways. Discernment is necessary. "You are the company that you keep." We can quickly become pulled into casual relationships with people we share a commonality with. However, be aware that not all these relationships call us higher to

God if they stunt our growth in Christ. God expects us to be light in our conversations and our relationships, even with people that are non-believers. This entails that we use the opportunity to be a witness about Christ to others, as this is a part of our call to be disciples.

These principles focus on actively pursuing two types of relationships: those that contribute to our spiritual walk and those to whom we can contribute, both believers and non-believers. That's not to say that fun can't be a part of it. Fun should be a considerable part of connecting and doing life with others!

When taking a look at my intimate circle of people, I would ask myself questions like:

Will this person go to the Lord on my behalf?

Will this person pray for me, my family, and our relationship?

Sometimes, it is not about the turn-up or good times that make relationships worthwhile because you will inevitably face trouble, struggle, death, and failure. Whom will you have to call upon other than the father himself?

Let us evaluate our connections and be intentional about those we share life with.

Home Front

We should be the beacon of hope for our kids and our household. One part of the Bible which has continually served as my guide on this journey of self-discovery is that which Solomon cited in the final part of Proverbs 31. Here, Solomon talked about the virtuous woman and all the qualities this great woman exemplified. We should want to keep our relationship with our household in high regard and keep out the things that may threaten the good things that we share within. We can often become overwhelmed with many things from different directions, especially in this time of modernization, where social media and other things have removed us from intimate, sincere connections with others. Our kids have become deterred and negatively influenced by what they see on TV, on social media, and in their everyday environments. These affect how they navigate life, just as it affects us. Still referencing Proverbs 31, we know that the woman provides for her family and protects her children at the due season, which is one crucial thing expected of us when living a life that impacts our immediate household. I learned that I had to Stabilize the walls of my household before trying to have an impact outside the home.

We should strive hard for God to be the primary point of discussion in the household by actively talking about God and sharing the great things that God has done for us. It's no longer "Do as I say, not as I do," because we should be the #1 influencer in our children's lives. That does not mean respect, honor, and discipline disappear; more so, God has entrusted us with precious beings, so we must be their light and first love. I would, at times, have "mom guilt' because I was a single mom always working and felt as if I didn't give the kids enough time. With the help of prioritizing and delegation, a set time with them, individually and collectively, became a necessity. Let us normalize learning and establish a middle ground that can work between parent and child when dealing with their hair, personality, and needs. A child is a person just as we were once a child. If it hurts, It Hurts. What gives us the right to strip away their ability to process emotions or voice uncertainty and pain? Our Children's Feelings Matter. In all, there is a need for us to set spiritual goals for the members of our household too. Old ways do not have to stay the same. Allow love to awaken dead routines.

Marriage

All titles come with a level of responsibility and sacrifice, so ensure you're willing to own them once you obtain them. Relationships come with disagreements. That is inevitable.

I don't believe Relationships were ever designed to be perfect. Why? In short, perfection isn't good enough. You have imperfect individuals pursuing one divine direction. If one reverts to old ways, so does the other eventually because they are threaded as one. For instance, if you go one way and he goes another, you two are living separately, unified. Until a Man searches the depths of His

Woman's Heart, I believe they will never cultivate and Reach Their Fullest Potential in Their Relationship. A man is called to love his wife as Christ loved the Church, which comes with a high degree of sacrifice and unconditional love. I believe that as a wife, it comes with a decision to be in alignment with your husband. Coming into alignment is not about losing who you are. Because your husband, whom God is leading, positions you as his missing rib, your submission will be ushered in naturally without force but through love. Two bodies are joined together as husband and wife in a blessed commitment. There isn't one without the other. When two cannot seem to coexist, magnets lose their pull, and separation occurs. Focusing on each other's shortcomings will drain your energy. Not saying ignore them entirely but think about what you need and communicate it. Breathe…Inhale, Exhale. Stop the stubbornness and nonsense at the door. <u>Grow</u> through it while you <u>Go</u> through it.

Let us talk.

That same love we give our spouse or partner, that same love we offer to our kids, that same love for our siblings and the people we connect with, is the kind of love we must give Ourselves.

All relationships, every single RELATIONSHIP, whether business or personal, will go through trials. It is up to us to allow the cycle of division to repeat itself or choose to break it and strive to be more unified. Allow Grace and Space to be present. You do care because We Must Care! Choose To Love.

Self-Love Is a True Love.

God's Love Triumphs Everything.

As women, we are natural-born facilitators of nurturing and care, but sometimes we independently take on more than what is assigned to us.

CHOOSE YOURSELF EVEN IF IT HURTS.

That deserves Intentionality.

Notes

Notes

Notes

CHAPTER 2:
LEARNING AND GROWING

Before I realized that my voice mattered in my relationship, I began to go on morning walks in my neighborhood. Morning soon turned into evening, and before I knew it, I was walking twice a day. I would get up early, read my Word, go for a walk, get the kids off to school, go to work, come home, cook dinner, and go for another walk. As time passed, my then-husband would not like that I finally had a life, a routine, and a space that did not revolve around him only. It was moments when it was just the good ole lord and me. I loved it there. There was peace, love, and protection.

On this journey of finding who I was in God's eyes, I learned that there is the need to move from one point spiritually to the other from time to time. There is no reward in being stagnant. For collaborative growth to occur in our lives, there must be continuously growing in the Word of God. Naturally, we might not notice any lack of spiritual growth living from year to year, but that is why it's essential to be cognizant of our walk with God. Growing in God's Word is a part of self-discovery by acknowledging where we are currently and where we should be measured by God's perfect will for our life. You'd be surprised how quickly years can pass by without memorizing one verse of scripture, not confronting habitual sin, not sharing the gospel with an unbeliever, or not experiencing conviction that lit a fire under you that caused you to live differently.

From the previous chapter, we have seen that in finding our path in life, we need to live a life of intentionality with our creator, ourselves, and those we connect with, which involves giving our all and not leaving any stones unturned. The race is not given to the swift or the strong but to the one who will endure to the end.

When I sat down with people I connected with, they usually said, "You seem to have it all figured out." But that was not true, as learning and growing is a long-term process. You never stop growing.

GETTING TO KNOW YOUR NEEDS

Do you seem to know what everyone around you needs more than your own?

It's time to break free from that. The focus is shifting to you now.

Every one of us has our own needs. I discovered that I needed to find out what I needed before I could fully invest in the needs of others. Without a Greater You First, there's no greater mom, wife, friend, or boss. Give yourself grace because this is a delicate process that requires all carefulness and diligence. I'm a farmer, so I look at things agriculturally in many aspects of life, so follow along with me. When plants are transplanted from one environment to another, a shock occurs. They appear to be limp, dead, or lacking something, and it seems as if there is a struggle for life. Eventually, they stand up and produce great fruit with proper nurturing and a solid strategy. Every plant has different needs, and it takes an in-depth study to know about the growth patterns and the most critical needs of every plant. It is the same for us. For our faith to grow, we must understand what best works for us. We all are unique in the presence of God, and He holds us in such high esteem that He knows the needs of everyone on Earth.

Getting to know yourself is just like getting to know another human being. You have to spend time with someone before you truly know them. Likewise, to get to know You, we must spend time with You –*daily.*

It may be awkward initially but understand that repetition creates habit, habit creates consistency, and consistency creates a lifestyle. Before you know it, you'll know yourself better than anyone else. Celebrate every little and big revelation of everything you will learn about yourself, your needs, and your ambitions.

When it is time to go…It is just time to Go. Gen 12:1-3

God told Abraham to go and separate from his country. I can imagine how hard it had to be to leave family, friends, and the place you call home, especially if happiness dwelled there. It is like the loss of someone or something. Grieving over someone still alive is hurtful (cuts deep), but being in covenant with God requires sacrifice. See, everything we walk away from is not always a bad thing... Sometimes, we must leave behind the good stuff, good job, good church, good friends, and good neighbors. Some will not recognize the purpose of your obedience, and that is ok. Stagnation and avoidable consequences are sure to follow if we don't move when it's time to move. You must grow... Grow in Christ, Grow in Relationships, Grow in Faith. Everyone else is not your responsibility at that moment.

The first time God told me to move from Texas, I did not listen, and those two years of disobedience cost me some things. I felt like my whole world turned upside down overnight, but then I heard a whisper, *"**My grace is sufficient.**"* God was preparing me in that in-between time. One thing about our God is that he will come a second time, just like he did for Jonah when he was in the belly of the whale. When God spoke that second time, I listened and saw how he had already prepared the way as I walked into the unknown on faith alone.

I remember having a packing party amid a worldwide pandemic. I hit up four women whom God had brought into my life for this very season. The relationships that God joins together are so satisfying and rewarding. The connection with these women helped me grow and see myself differently. I saw how alignment had brought something bigger into my life than I could ever imagine. It was a moment where once total strangers were now a sisterhood of women gathered, showing their love and support when it was needed the most. God is Good.

GOING DEEPER

Growing comes with going deeper in fellowship with God. This included me reading about God's Word, studying it to understand it, and being intentional about living a life of the two.

Question to self:
Where do I want to be in my relationship with the Lord by the end of the year?
Set tangible goals for getting there.

For instance, if you want to know God better, consider studying the history of the Old Testament and the life of Jesus in the New Testament. It's bigger than just setting a goal of reading the whole bible when usually, in the end, a box is checked with no added knowledge. To grow more profound, we must learn to set aside the good things to grab ahold of the best things.

Have you ever looked at a tree and seen the leaves growing and pleasing to the eyes? Eventually, limbs and leaves need to be cut down so that they do not overgrow, resulting in growth stunting. This process is called pruning. If we want to live for God, we need to allow ourselves to be pruned by God… the cutting off of dead or weighty things. Pruning is one of the most complex and painful processes a believer can undergo. Holding on to something God has ended will be painful. But I pray God gives you the strength to let it go gracefully. Accept that person, place, or thing has served its purpose in your life, and now it is time to gather your courage and walk into your next level.

As much as it depends on you, live peacefully with all. Let go so that you do not miss out by trying to preserve something that was never meant to last.

Seasons and Reasons... If a relationship no longer glorifies God but itself, it is Time. We must cut back to increase. We must say no to receive the yes. **No human can see all that hard work we put in beneath the surface, but God can.** God is proud of all you have done and are currently doing. Trust the process. It's worth it.

BUILDING ON A GOOD FOUNDATION

In varying conditions, foundations are vital. Foundations dictate how something or someone maintains during a shift. For example, how do we withstand things when things don't work out the way we figure they ought to? As believers, we must fabricate our lives on the foundations of the word, the lessons of Jesus, the messengers, and the prophets (Ephesians 2:19-22). On that foundation, we Stand!

Try not to NEGLECT THE FOUNDATION!

We must not forsake the wisdom of those that have come before us biblically or historically. We negate much if we are unwilling to accept the sound doctrine that aligns with the Word and the holy spirit.

Ponder and answer this question if you will:

- How solid is my foundation?

CONSIDER THIS . . .

"So why do you keep calling me Lord when you don't do what I say? I will show you what it's like when someone comes to me, listens to my teaching, then follows it. It is like a person building a house who digs deep and lays the foundation on solid rock. When the floodwaters rise and break

against that house, it stands firm because it is well-built. But anyone who hears and doesn't obey is like a person who builds a house right on the ground, without a foundation. When the flood sweeps down against that house, it will collapse into ruins. (Luke 6:46-49)

Even seasons of abundance need a solid foundation.

Wisdom: We can have it all, but we can't have it all at once if the foundation is not ready for it all.

Flawed and Bruised.

We all have had a place that required growth. Being born into sin signifies that there will be an error within us as long as we are in this earthly vessel. But because of Christ, sin dies, and resurrection takes place. Every rebirthing moment ushers in change.

"Change is the only constant in life." All seasons of life require a certain level of contingency to make it through. Your perspective shapes your decision-making. Every morning I rise, I thank the Lord for yet another day to walk in his Grace and Glory... Proclaiming, I give me YOU.

Logic is of the world by Man, not God.

Definition of Logic: a particular system or codification of the principles of proof and interference. However, there are no boundaries in God. God does the unexplainable and unattainable things that man cannot even fathom. His Power Can Not Be Measured, which is proven through the lives of his children.

Pivot... Assets do not measure success. It's the progress toward the standards God has set before us to follow. To keep moving forward, Stagnation cannot exist while piv-

oting. **Give complacency and Procrastination an eviction notice.** You are responsible for ensuring growth in every area of your life, whether mental, physical, or financial. "Faith is taking the first step even when you don't see the whole staircase." **Please repeat after me: Procrastination; you have to go!**

Are you trying to put a date on the perfect time to align with God?

Guess what? There is no perfect time. The time is now. Yes. Right where you are now. Yes, you can have peace and prosperity during a storm. Some moments cause us to look nowhere else but unto God himself.

Absolutely nothing is Too Difficult with God, yet we will still experience moments where we doubt God's ability to change our situation. Reciting affirmations such as, 'You are Chosen, and You are your Father's Child' reminds me of his limitless power when I look at what's in front of me versus trusting in his sovereignty.

There is no depth or height that God will not shake up for you. Victorious is YOU!

Notes

Notes

Notes

CHAPTER 3:

YOUR ONLY LIMIT IS YOU

A limit is a point or level beyond which something does not or may not extend or pass; a restriction on the size or amount of something permissible or possible. For instance, a 'speed limit' restricts a vehicle to a specific speed, even though the car was created to perform higher.

A limit is anything that restricts you from maximizing your potential.

In a particular season of my life, I would always tell myself, "I'm stuck in this mess I've created... God ain't gone get me out of this one." Words are powerful because, for years, I believed every word I spoke about my situation, ultimately limiting myself and the power of God to take place in my life. Fights are not won unless there is a tap out signifying that someone gives up... make sure that somebody isn't you! How you approach a situation can heavily determine if you will overthrow the odds.

Continuous Self-judgement can likewise restrict anyone from accomplishing or expanding beyond their capacity.

I recall finding myself asking questions such as:

Am I a good mother?

Am I in the will of God for my life?

Am I operating to my fullest potential?

Am I enough?

As I communed with God, I was led to extend myself grace just as I extend grace to others. That, in return, lessened my anxiety about things that did not align with the Word of God. Those unanswered questions would subside so I could hear what God was saying. Don't count yourself out and put seeds of 'less than' in your mind.

Free yourself from restriction. Your possibilities throughout everyday life start with adjusting your reasoning. Philippians 4:8-9 tells us, *Finally, brothers and sisters, whatever is true, whatever is pure, noble, right, lovely, admirable; if anything is excellent or praiseworthy; think about such things. Whatever you have learned or received or heard from me, or seen in me, put it into practice. And the peace of God will be with you.*

Knowing Your Spiritual Limits

God doesn't generally give us reasons why He restricts us profoundly.

Sometimes when we are slowed down, we are just being prepared for what's to come. While becoming, you must accept that there is an uncomfortable process along the journey. Just as Jesus died and rose again, there was a season between the Cross and the Resurrection. Before your renewed spirit fully manifests itself, you, like Jesus, will take many forms before you are at the Father's right hand. You, too, are HONORABLE.

Limited by Our Knowledge

The saying is true, "Knowledge is Power." Knowledge is life. If you want knowledge, read your bible. I also encourage you to read at least one book monthly, whether by turning pages or an audible one, but you must read. Knowledge is the awareness or familiarity gained by experience of a fact or situation. Pain is an excellent example of knowledge. Once you've experienced pain and healing, you have a different level of knowledge than before. For the knowledge of the Word to activate in our lives, we must meditate on it day and night. The Word gives us new insight or perspective in all situations. What the world presents as knowledge or clarity today may differ next year, but the Word forever stays the same.

In some cases, it is enticing to follow trends or famous thoughts; however, we generally need to test these against the Scriptures for exactness. "We talk where the Scriptures talk and stay quiet where they are quiet." Never place yourself in a position to stop learning from others. The information God has entrusted you to share with the world has done the same for others, so I say, "He who has ears, let him hear what the Lord may be speaking to you."

Limited achievement is debilitating and disappointing, yet never consider it God leaving or disregarding you - God is consistent with the holy people whether they are yelling from the mountain or battling in the valley.

You Are Worth It

John 10:10
The enemy comes to steal, kill, and destroy…but Jesus came so that we may have life and have it to the full.

Domestic violence has been one of the enemy's greatest weapons to limit people. You may or may not remember certain things as a child, but you will remember ABUSE. I was 11 years old when I was awakened by my mother shattering the living room coffee table. Did she fall? No. Her boyfriend was the cause. I did not know what was happening as a child, but I saw that momma was not having it. She picked herself up, took me by the hand, and we were out of there. Shortly after, we relocated to another city more than 400 miles away. Momma never looked back. In my head, maybe that was normal, but that led me to reflect on how I would later leave situations when trouble was stirred up. The pattern repeated itself in my adult life whenever a crisis presented itself.

See, kids mimic what they see regardless of if it is wrong or right because as a child thinks, so is he. I would proudly serve my country every day just to come home and catch a beatdown. I remember one day when my body was folded in a non-combative fighting position so that no bruising would be visible outside my Army uniform. After a nice dinner with wine, that same wine glass was used for my protection. I broke it by the stem to save myself from being beaten again.

Crazy, huh? I thought that the pain of my life was way over until ten years later, and by then, I had three beautiful children with a gun pointed at me. My son held a shirt to my blood-drenching eye as I prayed for my attacker not to kill me in front of my kids. Crazy, huh? What's even crazier is that I married him afterward. Talk about Stockholm Syndrome… I was in an actual, unhealed state of denial. Going to school to be a psychologist made me feel exempt from thinking I could ever be someone who couldn't decipher between feelings and reality. I would judge other women and say, "She is stupid; I could never." "How could she dare take him back after all of that?" Now, I was that woman, and because I didn't give myself time to heal or process my realities, I placed my kids and myself in a situation that would later result in years of healing. This time, it was not alcohol that would pull me out… It was not the next rebound guy. It wasn't even working myself to exhaustion. I've learned that those old vices that once worked in different seasons will not deliver me in this new season.

The Holy Trinity, Therapy, and My Support system brought me through. I chose myself, and I have never been the same. I found myself during all of life's chaos. I found God and a new world emerged before me where I could see that my steps were indeed ordered.

We Are in a Battle with This World

Although we are in a profound fight, we must utilize the weapons associated with each war to defeat the enemy with his unobtrusive gadgets. Using what God has given empowers us to "keep one stride in front of the foe," thus disappointing the enemy in his motivations when he comes against us.

How can we fight our spiritual battle well?

There are battles of perspectives within the world that frequently prompt believers to choose to follow Christ or Self-Proclaimed Gods. Battles inside the congregation involve bogus teaching—attempting to obliterate the herd. This is executed by evil spirits and the authorities of the darkness (Eph 6:10-13). The Christian life is a constant conflict; many don't make it. In the scriptures, Paul refers to three previous innovators in the congregation, Hymenaeus, Philetus, and Alexander, who wrecked the confidence of some believers. Their teaching would later lead to more ungodliness and iniquity.

What better thing to live and die for than the great conflict between God and Satan a battle for the spirits of people and the brilliance of God and our Savior? There could be no more meaningful work we can offer ourselves than taking on this conflict for individuals' spirits and God's magnificence. It is an acceptable battle. The way that Paul urges Timothy to face the conflict infers that it is feasible to battle well or not battle by any means. Tragically, this is the truth for some. Some get trapped in wrongdoing and quit progressing. Some fall head over heels for the world and things of this world and become dormant in sin. A few, by experiencing some trouble, get debilitated. Some get caught in bogus teachings. Many become lost because of at least one of these elements, never to return. This is genuinely a conflict that creates generations of purposeless lives. To win, we should drink profoundly from the Word and wear the whole Armor of God. Remember, there is no condemnation for those who are in Christ Jesus.

Awakened

You cannot win a fight in your opponent's territory unless you fight smart. Your prayers need to be different in these battles. Prioritizing God made me ask for wisdom. When fighting in the spirit, wisdom and revelation were some valuable tools.

"Lord, reveal what you need me to see and give me the insight to proceed accordingly."

We go through so many things in life that we may feel as if nothing can break us until something breaks us... Until that moment, we used to have all the answers or someone we could call to get the answers we sought. Sometimes, we even "deal with it" and think we are moving on with life as if it does not bother us. It is time to break that cycle of not dealing with the uncertainties of our lives. It is time to love your mental health. I even allow my kids to take mental health days away from school just as we take time off work. Remember, they are humans too. At those moments, we must realize that we must call on the name of our Father because when nothing else helps or gives us the clarity, peace, or love we need, he will come through and deliver us from whatever we ask of him. Angels surround you, and the Holy Spirit is never far away. Proclaim, I can do all things through Jesus Christ, from whom my true help comes! Trusting in that proclamation is Key.

If you have been called to carry something that has weighed you down for the last time, put on a back brace, steel-toe boots, sunglasses, and puncture-proof gloves, and get back into the fight!

The devil has stolen something from you, and you must get it back. It did not kill you, but you were robbed. Too late to switch up now and make it normal. Stand up and Win!

God is not man; that lies. Go after everything he promised you!

Stop for a moment... Do not allow the spirit of envy to create in you a person that you are not. You have no idea what a person has been through, prayed themselves through, or the miracle that saved their life to have them in this remarkable season of life they are in. Instead, celebrate with them because what God has for you is specifically for you. Someone else's walk may have cost them more than you are willing to pay. Just wait your turn.

Pick your fights because some are meant to be left alone. God knows all and sees everything! Nothing goes unnoticed or unpunished. Pray for those that hurt or avenge you. Channel negative energy for the preparation of an on-the-spot "Jesus Opportunity."

- An opportunity to save someone from committing suicide by speaking and holding a small conversation.
- An opportunity to bless someone financially, even if it's $5 for lunch or $20 for gas.
- An opportunity to help someone's self-esteem with a simple compliment of a fresh haircut or you have a beautiful smile.

Someone may need your encouragement today at work, at the grocery store, or at home.

Living in a consistent state of bondage will have you missing out on whom God created you to be before you were in your mother's womb.

Do you know who you are?

Have you seen that Giant in you that was in David?

Has an unexpected opportunity presented itself to you and blown your mind?

God is real and looks for people who bow before a sovereign king's throne. In a world where a moment of hurting is inevitable, I want you to know that our Father is an On-Time God. Hang in there... Push Through All the Motions. You are stronger than the enemy even knows. I am praying for you. Pressure Creates Character. The torch is on you because you have what it takes. Carry the load and press your way through. Alone you are not!

Notes

Notes

Notes

CHAPTER 4:

FORGIVE YOURSELF

The Enemy was my Inner-Me

Take a moment and examine that inner raging particle that lies within you... it's in all human beings. When emotions are louder than my thoughts, I proclaim that no weapon formed against shall prosper. God gives gifts in dark places.

Emotions can create uncalculated situations and circumstances, so we must intentionally hone in on them. Emotions can sometimes take a toll on our mind and body, but I say to you, never make decisions based on emotions. Please take a moment to digest all your emotions and sit with them before reacting. Pray and even fast if you must.

Sometimes it is not about what others think you should do but more about what God will lead you to do. Remember, some hasty decisions can come with a price we may not be willing to pay. The Bible says to be anxious for nothing but in everything by prayer and supplication. Being quick to listen and slow to respond is another gem of wisdom we should harbor in our minds and heart. Don't be afraid to stand alone when you're standing for what is correct. I must trust in God's infinite wisdom when my plans crumble, and I'm being taken away from my dreams. When my cup of suffering seems too much to bear, I must rest in his immeasurable love. I must remember God's sovereignty when my life spins out of control. I may not understand what is happening. But I refuse to stop talking, praising, or worshipping him. I must go to Jesus and tell him my doubts and ask for clarity and guidance.

Forgiveness is available to those who ask. God knew you would be walking into whatever you are in but be assured that he has never left the righteous forsaken. Absolutely nothing or anybody can ever love you and make you feel loved like Jesus. Sometimes, we must let go to move forward.

Reflection

You have so much love in that heart of yours... Now keep some for yourself. Your heart is like a banking transaction. Things flow In as well as Out. Do not allow your heart to go into Overdraft for the reason of... "You Have a Big Heart." A whole heart is not fulfilled by taking Chances hoping to be the winner in Tic Tac Toe. You have come too far to be locked back up in a shell of Safety. There is no progression in hiding. You are the light of the world, so Shine! -Matthew 5:14.

A lot is happening worldwide, yet time still waits for no man.

Be joyful in your future.

Be patient in your trials.

Be faithful in prayer.

God has it all under control.

The spirit is willing, but the flesh is weak. It is no unfamiliarity that fighting your flesh is one of the most challenging fights you endure daily. Denying yourself of things your flesh yearns for is so hard. Can I get an Amen? Human error will exist no matter what, so understand that fleshly ways can produce <u>uncircumcised capabilities, so</u> we must be careful about how we move.

-uncircumcised.

(Other **synonyms**: <u>unchristian</u>, irregular, ill-mannered, skeptical, unmannered, desecrate, unmerciful, raw, <u>crude</u>, <u>unconsecrated</u>, skeptical, unmannerly)

-Capabilities definition.

(The power or ability to do something).

Following your flesh will give you the power to be unchristian and unconsecrated. Today's believers commonly face the lust for the things of the flesh. This is because sin is humans' nature following Adam and Eve's fall in the Garden of Eden. This curse gave the flesh power over what we do, hence, temptation.

On my path with God, this is what I believe: Through the power of the Holy Spirit in my life, I can have victory on the inside. Without God, we don't stand a chance in this fight. With God, you can master your flesh. There is also the need to be aware of sinful patterns, as the fight is not against things seen but against powers and principalities. The enemy never rests. We must always be on Watch Guard and keep ourselves from providing everything the flesh seeks. Spirit over Flesh will only win if we spend more time in spirit than in the flesh.

Reflective Thought: Sometimes, we pray just to miss the answer. We pray day in and, at times, night out for God to show us what to do in a relationship. Red flags are thrown, and sometimes the damage is done. When the problem arrives, we fix it. Some flags are meant to be flown with the wind, and some are intended to burn like fire. Ashes are for the memories that you will keep. Do not miss it this time. Another flag has been called on the play, and that is enough to walk away Gracefully.

Sing songs of praise:

Day and Night, Night and Day, let incense arise!
I will always bless the Lord!
We all will fall short of the Glory of God, yet, **there is redemption in forgiveness.**

At some time and moment in our life, we must decide to deal with the fact that nobody else is responsible for our emotional well-being. Deal with your stuff and address your feelings with your big girl panties on. God will guide you and give you peace that surpasses all understanding. Be blessed and choose happiness. There is a difference between God's Given Peace and Pacification. Pacification creates non-confrontational individuals. When we petition Christ to go before us in a situation, the environment is prepared for us to act. Don't avoid what you have been praying for.

Elijah's journey began in private. God places us on a personal journey to heal or build us up for the next season. Take your healing and building as preparation for forgiveness. Never get too attached to people, places, or things because different seasons produce different fruits.

Writings on the wall: Rushing Waters

Feeling the waterthrush against your feet is powerful.

As powerful as the unknown of the deep blue seas.

Do you hear the sound?

The sound of the wind blowing, although you cannot see it...

Can you hear me now? Our Father calls out.

I need you just as much as you need me, to pursue the mission I have assigned to you. You will Conquer every battle you will face. The night falls quickly... terror by night, joy by day.

Note to Self:

Don't allow comfort, convenience, and familiarity to call you back to something God did not ordain. You must reconcile with your feelings.

Your emotions can get you into something you're not ready for.

Samson killed himself, innocent people, and more because of what?

His emotions.

SARCASTIC GOD

God said he is waiting on your yes for his power.

I was petitioned to walk out on Faith when it was time to be a full-time entrepreneur, trembling, you hear me! I had to repeat continuously; He would never leave me. He will never leave me. LOL.

So, I was introduced to a software company willing to help me Completely Free with website design, logo setup, and POS background understanding. I said to them, "What is the catch?' Ha-ha, due to being conditioned that if something sounds too good to be true, then it cannot be true. Being in alignment with God, however, there was no catch. The next day, I submitted my information to the company, ready to see what they came up with. I see the draft and realize, wow, I like it, but it's not representing my entire vision. Now, I have work to do that I never thought I could do because I had no knowledge of web design. God said, "So you thought I was going open the door, pay the price and let you do nothing? Ha-ha. Although this challenged me in many new ways, I helped build my first web page, free of charge... Look at God!

Not Looking Back

We say, "If I had known what I know now, it would all be perfect." Growing is not about perfection; it's about evolving. This new road that I am on, bumpy and twisty as it may be, is the path God has chosen for me. It is the best road. The only one worth taking. If I keep looking back on the old way longingly, focusing on what I've lost rather than what I have, I will miss the rewards of the new path. Be <u>in</u> the moment, not <u>of</u> the moment. I need to open my eyes. Notice what's around me. Remember that God goes before me. I need not fear, for he knows what is up ahead. As he has promised, ***"I will lead the blind in a way that they do not know, in paths that they have not known; I will guide them. I will turn the darkness before them into light, the rough places into level ground. These are the things I do, and I do not forsake them"*** (Isaiah 42:16).

God is guiding me on this new path. I am on the right road, and so are you.

It does not matter what is not working in your life or what is not right... What matters is what is working and what is right. Focus on those things. Make your request known and Put trust in God alone.

PRAYER: Father, I understand the area the devil attacks me the most is where You want to use me the most. I pray that you keep me covered by the blood of Jesus and give me strength where I am weak. I pray for Perseverance and Resilience through the day's journey and love to help heal the land. Thank you for life and connection. In all these things, I pray, Amen.

Revelation: Who cares what others think?

Just as a man will build you, man will surely tear you down.

God is the author of your life story.

Be still and know he is God!

God will make a way.

My God is a provider.

My God is not man; that lies.

My God is alive and doing big things in me.

Notes

Notes

Notes

CHAPTER 5:

THE NEW THING

Cycle of Life

God takes us through cycles to help us learn ourselves. If we don't know who we are, we'll never know how we ought to live. The first thing that happens when we give our lives to Christ is that God gives us a new identity.

Once, we were separated from God because of our sins – and not just separated, but alienated from Him. The Bible says we were "excluded, without hope and without God in the world" (Ephesians 2:12).

After your commitment, a new relationship can begin to evolve. He is now your loving heavenly Father, and you are now His child, spiritually reborn into the Kingdom.

Transformations occur in those moments that only trial or tribulation could birth. There is a process in everything in life... The God of Order. Everything Shall Work Out for The Better Good. God is my fortress and has given me new life. This was exemplified in the Psalms of David, where God transformed his adversity and transgressions into something of joy.

Some people are very focused, using their energy to reach their goals. Others drift through life with little purpose or direction, living for the moment and never thinking about where they are headed. Most people live somewhere in between. But they all have this in common: They live only for themselves and their happiness.

But when we come to Christ, God gives us a new purpose.

Now we want to live for Christ and not just ourselves.

A New Life is one of God's promises to us, and we know that **all His promises are fulfilled**. As believers, our hope ultimately rests in the assurance that Christ will return for us one day and make *all* things new (Revelation 21:5).

The 'There' and 'Now'

Miracles are still happening every single day. Give me this day, my daily bread, oh God. Daily... Worry not about the cares of tomorrow, for tomorrow already has its troubles. I will call on the name of the Lord!

As I embarked on this new journey, I had to forgive myself when my ignorance made a choice. Yes, sometimes we even know better and still do the opposite.

As a novice in gardening, I would plant seeds and wait for them to grow. Some crops would die, and Some would sprout and still die.

Once you plant a seed, I have learned that the environment matters. You cannot plant a seed without proper germination and expect a great harvest. You cannot plant seeds too close to others, or there will not be enough room for them to grow to their full potential. Lastly, if the depth of its environment is too shallow, it will only grow to its restricted growth point.

The Environment of the Seed you plant is Important.

2 Corinthians 9:10

Reflect

Do not get into something new before becoming somebody new.

'A fool is as a fool does.' Do not allow hasty decisions and a racing heartbeat have you wearing your heart on your sleeve from a foolish decision.

Being down bad may not be considered bad to them, but remember, it does not matter how others weigh your downs; it is how you measure up to them!

You were not designed to figure it all out. If you can figure out the answers to all your questions about why something is happening, it's not GOD anyway. It is not for you to know what He is up to but, more importantly, to know you are more than a conqueror because greater is He within you than He who is in the world.

Seasons Change... So Should YOU!

Isaiah 43:18-19

Forget the former things; do not dwell on the past. See, I am doing a new thing!

"Depending on where you sit, determine what you see, and what you see determines what you do!"

Some are having pity parties, but you are having a praise party because you understand that not everyone deserves you, which is ok.

There will be Seasons of ambiguity where you must advance without answers—just Faith. It's Seasons where you must move on without closure. If God has not given you an answer now, you do not need an answer right now and must move on anyway. You will not know that God is all you need until you are in a situation where God is all you got!

Be careful to produce fruit in getting ahead of God. That Does not mean it will stop you from getting to where God is taking you, but it will make things more complicated than they had to be. As soon as you can come to terms with what was no longer is, you will begin to experience the new things God has waiting for you to walk in.

When it was time for me to take off my Chef hat and pursue a full-time farming life, I was not happy at all. I had a big tantrum. I would yell at God, "But all I know is Cooking; why are you calling me out of something you called me into?" I had been learning how to farm vs. gardening for only a year vs. the ten years of being a chef and having a successful catering business. I eventually let go and let God show me something valuable: Just because one thing ends at the beginning of a new thing does not mean it dies forever. I now see how my long-lost dream of being a farm-to-table Chef correlates to why I had to temporarily take off that chef hat and break up with that path. Becoming one with earth, seeing mother nature perform, and meeting souls of likeness has produced nothing short of the plan of God. My son would come to do outdoor meditation and water yoga. My middle daughter found drawing healing by simply sitting by the water. My youngest daughter gained her favorite attribute, resilience while learning how to grow her food and teach others to do the same. We all found a piece of ourselves by being where we didn't desire to be yet trusting the process. Trust God's plan... rewards are waiting just for you.

JOURNAL ENTRY

Dear Shawn, this phase of love has taught you that you can be vulnerable, loving, caring, and submissive. You have become a woman you never knew — a virtuous woman of true strength and perseverance through the many transformations by Jesus Christ. When you welcomed God in, he began to change your entire being. You no longer allow the things you used to stand for because you came to see who you are. Your perspectives were altered, and you became a better person. You are now walking on a path of Faith. You have no idea what your future holds, but you believe God is working it out for your good. Lashawndra, thank you for being obedient to the call. He who has ears, let him hear. Let God shake your world up; he knows his plans for you. You are God's gift, and he handles you with care. Press and stand on the promises of God, for His ways are not your ways, nor are His thoughts. Trust in Him Always. You better act like you know that you do not have blind faith, for you have experienced miracles for yourself.

Reminder: You are all that and a whole bag of baked potato chips!

I HAVE NEVER SEEN THE RIGHTEOUS FORSAKEN
Psalms 37:25

I have been young, and now I am old; yet, I have never seen the righteous forsaken nor his seed begging for bread.

The saying goes: Time heals all things. On the contrary, that is not true for all things. Time does not necessarily heal all wounds, but time will teach you how not to allow that thing, situation, or circumstance to keep you in a repeated cycle of self-destruction.

Going through life, I have learned that after many knockdowns in various areas of life, with love and time combined, those two ingredients have a way of working some things out. That applies to life, relationships, work, emotions, death, anxiety, losing people, etc.

At this very moment, if you can, reflect on how love and time have brought you out of places that no man, therapy, drinking, clubbing, or busyness could have ever brought you to.

Sometimes we live surrounded by many people, yet still feel alone because there is an unknown inner issue that we could be suffering from, like...

Trust Issues... Heartbreak... Abandonment from a parent.... Losing everything... Grieving... Over-Excelling... Under-Achieving... Cycles....

Or times when God's vision does not match our reality.

God loves you unconditionally and will never leave nor forsake you when you need him most. That is LOVE. He knows how much our Strong Selves can bare and will save us when we call upon his name.

Allow your faith to be activated and witness your deliverance!

BEFORE I FORMED YOU, I KNEW YOU
Jerimiah 1:5

Before I formed you in the womb, I knew you. Before you were born, I set you apart; I appointed you a prophet to the nations.

That verse made me go, "YOU KNEW ME?" I thought my momma and my daddy... just joking...ha-ha-ha. The Father knew us before our parents even hooked up to put us being born into motion. Once I started believing in those scriptures, My Life Changed. I have always dipped and dabbled in and out of the church, but I was consistent this time. Every Sunday and eventually Wednesday, I was there, yearning for more and more of his Word to be interpreted so that I could understand and become more and more in relationship with this God that has me feeling like... There Has to Be More to Life Than

This. Growing up and even in my adult life, I never knew I could have a relationship, a bond, with this God we sing and pray to. Once you experience the presence of God, where the Holy Spirit consumes you until tears run down your face, with visions of revelations revealed to you; Your soul never wants to be without that presence again.

Unlock the Blessings

In receiving God's blessings, we need to position ourselves properly so that God can bless us. I remember asking myself, "What if God wants to shower his blessings on me, but I'm not in the right posture?"

The book of Hosea 4:6 talks about this point which says that God's people suffer and go through pain because of their lack of knowledge.

Talk to God about the areas that seem to be an issue, where you tend to be suffering, and then ask Him to show you the light that will propel you toward going higher.

Unlocking God's blessings also entails that a person realizes that the choice of getting the benefits is theirs and not anyone else's. God has given us free will to choose between good and evil, and He has advised us, as illustrated in Deuteronomy 30:19-20.

The blessings naturally flow when you consciously honor God and follow His injunctions. Positioning yourself for the blessings of God requires you to get rid of any unbelief you may be shouldering. The word tells us that He is a reward for those that diligently seek Him. Trusting in God is an essential factor that helps to confirm one's blessings from God. Trust in the Lord, and He shall bring it to pass.

Ultimately, to unlock the blessings of God, we need to have a significant level of humility because God only deals with humble people. In fact, without humility, it is just as fruitless as planting seeds and eating unripe fruit. Therefore, humble yourself to be exalted.

Light Switch Moment

I remember standing in the rain with my Friendster, saying, "Can you hear it? The roaring thunder from up above?

Some say it was lightning…Some say it was thunder… Could there be a war going on in the heavens or, better yet, God speaking directly to us as he spoke to Moses?

This is what was revealed to me. God has never lost a battle. And now, as we wait, still struggling to make sense of the storms in our lives, let us pray as our Savior did. Let us draw near to God, believing He can grant peace while submitting our will to His. Our Father's plans are always divine. Give God the invitation to change the things we long to be different. Breathe. Observe where you are so that he can meet you in the darkness. You will find comfort in his presence.

A Moment of Thanks -Saving Me

When I Think About It All…

I Thank God Every Single Day for Creating and Saving Me.

To Have Someone I've Never Met in The Physical, Love Me Through All My Mess Unconditionally.

Inhale…Exhale… Breathe… This is just the beginning.

When I take a moment to Admire Myself, I see so much beyond the Beauty… I see Resilience; I See Truth; I See Strength; I See Growth. I Thank God for Saving Me. As I Evolve More and More Every day, Life has many perspectives that counterbalance and shape my World. When you love yourself, it makes it much easier for someone to love you back. I Thank God for placing me on such a humbling journey that has helped me evolve in many areas of my life. We always Win with God.

My God, I Thank You for pushing me to **Do the hard things!**

PRAYER: **Ask, and you shall receive.**
Lord, lead me not into temptation, convict me of my weakness, and be my strength in the fights I cannot win without you.

It might look like I am not paying attention, but I notice everything.

I love people, yet I still need time to recharge so that my higher self retains its value. Just because I carried this last season of my life well does not mean it was not heavy... Going through three divorces can create all kinds of negative thoughts that would plague me and leave me feeling like giving up on love. I am a witness that there is life and fullness of joy even after the death of something that once was good.

How do I know?

Because there is always a resurrection after death, I get the opportunity to live in it, alive and whole, every day, and so can you!

We must have Prayers to cover the men of God as well.

God! Raise up your Kings, your men whose hearts beat after you.

Ladies, we are to be helpmates, so encourage your brother, uncles, son, and all the men you are connected to. You may be the only voice of encouragement and power they encounter or experience. Be that healing voice because we know they have enough voices in this world that only try to tear them down. **Amen?** Amen

Your lens predetermines what your truth is, which is why there are often different perspectives.... that is what makes us all different. It is ok that we all may not agree on everything, vote for the same person, or move how other moves because we all share that one thing: We All Want the Kingdom to Reign!

Reminder:

Jesus died on the cross so that we all may have eternal life! Hallelujah

I may never be the same, but I will be whole.

Notes

Notes

Notes

CONCLUSION

Matthew 5:14-16 (NIV)
¹⁴ "You are the light of the world. A town built on a hill cannot be hidden. ¹⁵ Neither do people light a lamp and put it under a bowl. Instead, they put it on its stand, giving light to everyone in the house. ¹⁶ In the same way, let your light shine before others, that they may see your good deeds and glorify your Father in heaven."

1.) Jesus compares us to Himself.

He informs us in verse 14 that We are the world's light, just as He says He's the light of the world in John 8:12. Jesus is teaching us that we are identical to Him!

This revelation is astounding because as we shine our light in the darkest places here on earth, it will be evident that God is working through us and lives within us.

2.) You must shine the light wherever you go.

The globe requires it. When Jesus mentions putting a light under a table, He implies that if you have something that can benefit others, you should make it available so that others might benefit too. In other words, you must not keep your relationship with Jesus a secret.

Consider what would happen if Jesus wasn't Jesus.

What if Jesus came to this earth knowing everything there was to know about God and what the world required, but He chose not to communicate the Good News?

Wouldn't our world be very different if that happened? That isn't only true of Jesus.

Do you have a favorite author, pastor, family member, or friend? What if they didn't tell you about God's light in their life?

It is critical that you comprehend this.

Are you aware that you are one-of-a-kind?

Nobody else compares to you.

You are distinct, influential, and unique.

You are different; no one else was designed to be like you.

What you do has an impact.

Your purpose is significant.

We tend to see Jesus as a carbon replica of whom we are supposed to be, but we don't believe this could be the case for us for the following reasons:

1.) Jesus' mission and life had a special calling like ours. Jesus' call was not the same as yours or mine. Similarly, my call differs from yours.

Consider it in the context of a suncatcher. When the sun shines through several prisms, different colors are reflected. The angle of the light that enters through is the same. Although the light is always the same, how it is projected varies.

Similarly, we all have a similar calling from God – it comes from the same light source – but it manifests itself in various ways as it touches us.

2.) Paul's and Peter's ministries differed considerably from Jesus's. The ministry grew out of a personal relationship with Jesus yet celebrated people's differences. Furthermore, like the disciples, we have all had distinct experiences with God. We are shaped and informed by that experience because of God's presence and action in our lives, which make our walk and testimony different. Instead of losing our individuality, we enter a more sanctified, cleaner version of ourselves.

You are responsible for communicating what Jesus has done for you and in you to the rest of the world. Embrace Christ's love and allow it to guide your words, decisions, and actions. You are the light and the salt on your job, in your neighborhood, at the market, and inside the schools. You do not have to wait until life after death to experience the fullest of God's Glory. You can walk and possess a portion of the Promised Land here on Earth.

Sis, you are Righteous. You are Holy. You are Pure. Keep a heart of gratitude for all your supplications. Now that you realize you lost your voice and forgot who you were, It's Time to Reintroduce Yourself. You were once voiceless until You went and got it back.

Say This Out Loud:

I have a New Voice To be Heard.

A New Call To be Audacious.

For I am She, and She is Me!

Notes

Notes

Notes

REFERENCES

Bible.
NIV, NLT, AMP Versions

Rodney, W. F. (2004)
Building on a Good Foundation.

Bingham, G. (2008)
Discovering your identity.

Risner, V. (2016)
The Scars that have shaped me.

Mckie, Y. (2017)
Adversity Creates Purpose: Turning Pain into Prosperity

Smith, R. (2019)
Faith on Friday: A Deeper Dive

Boykin, K. (2020)
How to Practice Intentional Living. Hello Sensible

Ann, M. (2020)
Living Intentionally for God. Busy Blessed Woman.

ABOUT THE AUTHOR

Being by water, taking nature walks, and listening to the sounds of the wind is what I call a good time. I tend to remain calm and realistic to have a wise temperament when dealing with others. I love the clarity and may strive to ensure success by following a strict plan. I have a naturally keen eye for errors and a strong urge to correct them. These qualities contribute to my balance in life. I have this thing where I 'O.A.E,' Observe, Analyze and Execute.

Before starting something or speaking a word, I use this strategy to make a calculated decision, but I have not always been that way. When things in my life would get tough, I would have all kinds of what-if possibilities that plague my mind, yet I remind myself to breathe and stay optimistic. We all have a life story that will highlight our successes, struggles, and failures. As an infant, I was given up for adoption, raised in poverty, experienced my mother's death at age 14, became a troubled and runaway teen, and was a high school dropout. I've served my country honorably in my adult life, graduated from college, went through marriage, divorced three times, birthed three brilliant little humans, built a relationship with my biological parents, and experienced traumatic yet redeeming moments. I was never taught how to stand up for myself, embrace change, or how to tackle difficult times strategically. Yet, it was instilled in me that it was always better to give than to receive and that simple conversation could change the lives of those around me.

Twenty-one years later, I would finally understand the meaning of what my mother would tell me before she transitioned, "Never be afraid to start over as long as you move forward."

Living as a daughter of the Most High has brought me into a lifestyle of purposeful freedom that I get the opportunity to live out every day.

Feel free to follow Lashawndra at:

www.allthingslashawndra.com

www.ingramcontent.com/pod-product-compliance
Lightning Source LLC
Chambersburg PA
CBHW060330050426
42449CB00011B/2713